A Little Exercise for Young Theologians

Helmut Thielicke

Translated from the German by

Charles L. Taylor

WILLIAM B. EERDMANS PUBLISHING COMPANY
GRAND RAPIDS, MICHIGAN

Wm. B. Eerdmans Publishing Co.
2140 Oak Industrial Drive N.E., Grand Rapids, Michigan 49505
www.eerdmans.com

22 21 20   34 35 36

ISBN 978-0-8028-7415-3

A LITTLE EXERCISE
FOR YOUNG THEOLOGIANS

Contents

CONTENTS

Introduction

Think, if you will, of this modest book as if it were a greeting card. It can serve best in its first purpose: as a *bon voyage* greeting to a person venturing for the first season into theological studies. Just as well, the book could say "Happy Anniversary" to a practical parson humble enough to look back, to measure him- or herself against his or her intentions. Then, again, it may be needed as a "Get Well" where there is hope for a pretentious theologian or — in radical instances — as a sympathy card to someone who has forgotten the whole excitement and promise of the theological task.

In the paragraph I have just written, some version of the term "theology" appeared three times.

Thus it carefully reproduces the intention of the book: in clear and forceful language the author sets out to speak of the difficult language of theology. If it is used to greet a young theologian, the book will not soon be placed back among his or her souvenirs. To begin to exhaust its meanings, one must consult it again and again. The author expects the budding theologian to take from it good counsel.

Before anyone accepts counsel one naturally does well to examine the credentials of the counselor. By what right does he speak? Will he preach at me or insinuate his opinions into my consciousness? Will he pontificate or will he be condescending? In this instance, does he know what theology and young theologians are all about?

Concerning few people in the Christian world would one have fewer hesitancies than we reserve for Helmut Thielicke. He wore several mantles, and they fit well. As Rector of the University of Hamburg he was obliged to wear the business suit of the secular administrator — as he calls himself in these pages — as well as the historic academic garb of that post. As a practicing theologian, he wore the robes of professorial office in order to provide the setting for a learned lecture on Christian ethics. Most readers could picture him best in his preaching robe: some number him among the greatest preachers of the twentieth century. It is well known — the covers of German news magazines testified — that he filled a very large church in "secularized" Hamburg twice a week. His translated sermons, running into a number of volumes, are among the few that preachers read for their own nourishment. Finally, we picture him as world-traveler or storyteller in his corduroy sport coat. He was at home in all these roles; each equipped him for the tones of voice he uses here.

A scholarly, intense, concerned man, Thielicke wins the confidence of his hearers. He says some things to young theologians here which few other people could say with such sting and still such grace and healing. No doubt in the ozoned reaches of Continental theology there are more astute theologians than he. No doubt in the broad pavements of American practical church life there are better administrators. But few are his peers for synthesizing respectable scholarly inquiry and informed practical church leadership. The synthesis is sorely needed in Europe today and I am sure it is equally welcomed, from a different angle, in the Western hemisphere.

Born in 1908, pursuing a conventionally broad and deep German theological education, Thielicke underwent a personal crisis in the 1930s. Then, as his career blossomed, he was to be tried by the terror of National Socialism. He won a new kind of right to speak by his opposition to Nazism. After World War II he came to prominence. Experienced theologians or parsons who pick up this book will no doubt already have on their shelves several of the titles which reveal his range of interests: *Between God and Satan, The Silence of God, Our Heavenly Father, The Waiting Father, How the World Began, Christ and the Meaning of Life, Nihilism,* or his informed reply to Rudolf Bultmann. The newcomer to theology will soon be possessing and reading these as well as plowing through his massive *Theological Ethics*. Thielicke wrote as rapidly as some of us read.

The biographical accent of these first pages is not intended to embarrass the author, but to show how the particular set of virtues he combined is rarely come by, sorely needed, and essential for the task before him: the giving of advice. I should not wish to make it seem that theology is to him a superficial task in either the intellectual or moral sense. You will see him define it as "reflection" on the one hand, or as "conscience" on the other. His work reveals an inner consistency that certifies the impression that Thielicke's many expressions come from one radiating center.

Of course, the author's assets bring with them certain liabilities. His overpowering style sometimes obscures the validity of alternate viewpoints. For instance, his Christian consciousness prematurely overpowers the nihilist whom he would understand in his book on nihilism. Or, again: one can read his exegesis of a parable and be awed by it. Then, on consulting the text and the various other careful inquiries concerning its meaning (say, in Joachim Jeremias or Charles H. Dodd), a student may become convinced that "scientifically" the others may be more faithful to the parable. Thielicke's intuition and instinct are so colorful that other levels of interest and accuracy may suffer. You may ask, "Why fault Thielicke for the intensity of his analysis and expression?" Still, it is possible that a person of great consistency and articulateness will have an unfair advantage over those who bring quieter theological disciplines to their task. The reader can make the test him- or herself; the publishers provide clean margins for notes and arguments. A book of advice should be taken that way.

Dr. Thielicke calls this "A Little Exercise for Young Theologians"; in it he goes about his assigned task of opening a seminar in his own discipline. The publishers have, I believe wisely, kept the work's personal character in mind. They have retained a number of references which mean less to an American audience than to the original hearers. But thus we get a sense of eavesdropping on a lecture we should like to have attended in person. This removes the sense that we might be offered here some gratuitous advice. In naming this an "exercise" Thielicke has in mind the format of Loyola's *Spiritual Exercises* and other books of Christian self-discipline. That is how I would describe this book: it is a lesson in theological self-discipline. It may be only a "little exercise" in a profound field; it may be *Eine kleine Nachtmusik*, or a grace note alongside the *De Profundis* of the theological library, a pen-sketch to be left at the foot of the mural. But in its modest way it can inform the whole. An "aside" whispered in a stage play can deal a glancing blow to every other direct line. Here is Thielicke's aside to a theological audience.

A temptation often comes to one who introduces a book to anticipate or repeat its contents. Instead, I would rather converse with its argument. Does the Christian who is becoming or has become a self-conscious theologian in America have the same problems as those cited here? On the Continent — so it is said — the theologian lives more in the ivory tower than does his or her American counterpart; the activist there is less activistic; theology there has less to do with the life of the church than with rigorous, scientific, respectable discipline. In evangelism, stewardship, pastoral care, administration, the American church leader heads the field.

But the conventional picture is changing. German theologians were flushed out of their towers by the courage called forth in Hitler's era, and they have not been allowed to return because of the challenge to relate the faith to a secularized world after. Meanwhile, the European parson has had to work harder to gain attention, to hold and minister to his or her flock.

In America the twenty-first-century theologian has a similar task. The theologian does not speak only to the theologian but to the "outsider." The practical church leader may have it easier — at least in a superficial sense — than the Continental colleague who experienced less religious revival. The day has come, however, when we must speak of difference in degrees, not in kind, between the intentions of theologians and the intentions of parish ministers on both sides of the Atlantic.

Despite the lessened tension, a tragic breach remains between theological ventures and activist programs, between the communities and persons who support them. Seldom does the lay congregation recognize or trust the worth of academic theology. Seldom do the academic theologians empathize with the workaday parsons. Now Christianity allows for a variety of gifts, with the same spirit. Some of these gifts must be allowed for and encouraged in the same people. Thielicke argues that every minister of Jesus Christ must be both a disciplined theologian and a practicing church leader. That is another concern of his little exercise.

Independent of Thielicke's outline I have tried to think what are the enemies of theology in America. First is the pervasive unbelief that makes its way into academic circles. It motivates the counsel to avoid theology, counsel which says: the Christian faith cannot pass intellectual tests; therefore keep busy, do not subject Christian affirmation to analysis and scrutiny, and it may survive. Second is an apathy or low imagination extended to many crucial ventures of the church. If something does not immediately seem to affect what goes on within the walls of my church tower, the confines of my parish, I do not often care. Still another enemy is the idolization of the "doer" as opposed to the "thinker." The Big-time Operator or the Good Joe somehow builds more buildings, raises more budgets, preaches louder sermons than does the artisan who pores over the Greek New Testament. It is of little consequence to some that this type contributes to a greater divorce between Christ and the meaning of life, between the faith and other verities. So long as the engines puff and the wheels roll, all is well. Finally — I hesitate to make too much of this — there is an anti-intellectualism in American religion, a legacy of nineteenth-century concerns for pious and warm hearts for God; or anti-intellectualism may be a by-product of twentieth-century generalized religion with its relativism.

Whoever wishes to do these exercises in America should also, if he or she follows Thielicke's rules, empathize with the enemies of theology. There are reasons for mistrust, the first being the frustration occasioned by its limits. Theology cannot always deliver. It cannot answer where the revelation does not ("What is the ontological origin of evil?" etc.). At other times, false claims made for the intellect alienate pious Christians. Eunomius, Bishop of Cyzicus in the fourth century ("I know God as well as he knows himself"), has too often seemed to be the patron saint of theologians. The well-known *odium theologicum*, the pettiness of little people who care much about big issues, is a proverbial problem. The tendency to abstract one's self from church life and concrete concerns often represents to laypeople and parish ministers of activist bent a tragic misreading of the Christian faith. The fact that theologians change their opinions as they learn more and experience more sometimes causes mistrust, though it should not: complete truth belongs alone to God. No doubt the most criticized fault of all is the specialized vocabulary, the shorthand, the jargon developed by theologians. We welcome technical terms in medicine (who wants just a stomach ache?), in science (where any child can spit out "world-wide web"), but we mistrust it where the simple gospel is concerned. Thielicke has wise words on this.

Despite the enemies of theology, despite the legitimate reasons for their mistrust, a theological necessity is laid upon the church. There is a mandate: love the Lord "with all thy mind." There is a changing world which presents ever new problems, basic new questions of language and meaning. Shall one build a tiny corral or a high wall around the faith, or shall one relate it to larger questions? The theological task possesses an intrinsic character: depth demands witness. There will inevitably be theology: will it be good or bad, conscious or unconscious, disciplined or diffuse?

Whoever cares about the American setting of problems such as these will welcome the translation of Thielicke's advice. We are in danger now of letting the envelope grow larger than the greeting card, or of cluttering with props the arena where the exercise should begin. The temptation to carry on prolonged dialog is hard to resist. Spiritual exercises call for response, arguments, commitment. If they awaken similar temptations in the minds of other readers, be they theologians or not, young or not, this book will have served its purpose.

— MARTIN E. MARTY
Chicago, Illinois

I

A Preliminary Understanding
with the Reader

(Originally with the Student in the Classroom)

Johann Tobias Beck, the old professor at Tübingen, now and then used to interweave asides into his lectures, thereby transforming the lecture platform into a pulpit. In my opinion, something similar cannot hurt us teachers and students of the present day. As often before, I am attempting here excursi of this kind. The reader will kindly understand this fact and be lenient about it, because these *obiter dicta*, both in form and content, are very sharply to be distinguished from the style and matter of formal lectures in theology itself. Keep in mind that such digressions must necessarily be spoken off guard, while the lecture proper cannot dispense with the rigors of its method nor with its safeguards.

Now and then, I believe, I must see and hear my listeners not only as students but also as souls entrusted to me. And this soul of a theological student is in great danger, by no means today only, but perhaps especially today. This is the subject matter of what follows.

Perhaps through these reflections a practicing parson may not only revive memories — though he surely will do that too! — but he may also feel himself addressed in his concrete theological predicament, as I in any event have intended to deal with my own. Possibly, out of sight of a theological professor, the practical brother in his pastorate may find in these remarks an explanation for, or a clarification of, strange conduct on the part of a theological student or of an inexperienced assistant. He may, therefore, understand what follows as a kind of little report, on what is happening today in our theological halls. But perhaps much will apply to himself too, and penetrate within the confines of his own study.

It is a commonplace we hear, and countless times have ourselves expressed, that theology has to do with life. This being so, it is only natural to begin with a meditation on how things stand with our Christian life in the midst of our course in theology, and how that life fares inside the race track of theological study — and not only fares, but how it can be made deeper, richer, and more fruitful.

Please understand this booklet as a little spiritual exercise with which I should like to preface the course itself, and which occupies a place in theology as a whole similar to that of the spiritual meditation and prayer which Anselm puts at the outset of his speculations in his *Prologue*.

2

The Anxiety of the Ordinary Christian about Theology

If Rudolf Otto said once that the Holy was not only fascinating but awesome (both *numen tremendum* and *numen fascinosum*), the same could be said also, with a grain of salt, of theology: for many it is awesome.

The ordinary Christian of a live congregation — that spiritual counterpart to the so-called man on the street — fears theology for several reasons. There is perhaps hardly a theological student who has not been earnestly and emphatically warned by some pious soul against the dubious undertaking of approaching Holy Scripture with scientific tools, against studying all "doubtful questions," and against casting himself into the arms of that omnivorous octopus, the unbelieving professor. Here I need only to appeal to your memories. What lies at the root of these warnings, these anxieties of the quiet in the land that forever trouble us?

The ordinary Christian does not wish to go into the question as to why the Word of God should be approached in any other dimension than that of the simplest faith, supported by no intellectual crutch — no pride in the wisdom of the world — why, in other words, any special armor "in addition to" faith is necessary. The earlier in the course of theological study that this question is raised, the easier it is to smile at these naive objections, and the more likely the student is to identify himself proudly as a member of the esoteric clique of the initiated. He may even feel that ordinary Christians just do not understand certain things, for example, the questions about the historical-critical study of the Bible, and that they cannot be explained to them. If the theologian, however, does not take more seriously the objections of the ordinary washerwoman and the simple hourly wage earner, and if he then thinks — he would hardly express it this way — that the spiritual proletariat is not aware of the delicate questions and must have nothing to do with them — which is just the way of that esoteric club — surely something is not right with theology.

If, in short, the so-called ordinary congregation is somewhat skeptical about theology, this skepticism is by no means naïve. It is supported, without doubt, by arguments from principle and from experience. And because we as theologians are all confronted with this problem — for insofar as we are determined to be true theologians, we think within the community of God's people, and for that community, and in the name of that community — how shall I say it? — we think as a part of the community itself — and because this very community is concerned very rightly for our spiritual health, I would like briefly to examine this matter.

3

Unhappy Experience with a Theologian's Homecoming

I said that the simple folk of the church could use arguments from experience and from principle. First let us consider the arguments from *experience*.

In order to impress you with this kind of consideration, I must be drastic and picture for you an event which may not be unfamiliar to you all, which moreover is repeated with sad monotony in many variations, and which the especially competent youth-pastor of Essen, Wilhelm Busch, reported to me in his own way with a kind of wry humor.

Picture a lively, active young man on good terms with his fellows in the youth work of his church. He has met Jesus Christ and now must bear witness. And so he is already occasionally leading devotions, for which he does not study commentaries, although he is careful enough to go through the printed aids which are available for such purposes, and he perhaps asks his pastor a question or two. For the rest he prays that God will grant him a right understanding of everything and keep him from speaking nonsense.

Whatever is derived from lively faith is itself lively. And so the young people are impressed. Moreover, the young leader is happy about his study of theology, because he fosters the hope that it will lead him deeper into the Bible and enlighten him on much that he now finds obscure. He is happy to be engaging in a calling in which his chief business puts him in touch with what he loves. Who would not be happy to live after his heart's desire!

When he comes home after his first semester, in the eyes of his former companions he has suddenly and horribly changed. If one of them, the young artisan, conducts Bible study that is highly lay in character, there he sits with the corners of his mouth drawn down. On their way home together afterward he explains to him — like a gossip who is almost bursting under the weight of her news — what "the latest investigation" has produced on the subjects of myth, legend, and form-history.

And even before the other has recovered from his momentary horror, he classifies him by that clerical typology that he has picked up in the lobby of his lecture hall. He says to his unlearned friend: "What you said was 'typically pietistic,' or 'typically orthodox,' or maybe 'Methodistic.'" He says to him: "You belong to the school of Osiander, which has not yet comprehended the forensic character of justification," — and he patronizingly explains to him the strange learned words, which are the questionable by-products of his scientific study.

When he comes home after his third semester — meanwhile his friend is too embarrassed ever again to launch his naive exegesis in the presence of those profoundly knowing ears — he is invited to tackle a Bible-study hour himself. Every choral society is naturally curious in the highest degree to see how one of its members, who meanwhile has been hav-

ing his tenor voice trained at an academy of music, is
going to sing on his first visit home. The disappoint-
ment is very frequently boundless: under a mighty
display of facial contortion and perspiring gesticula-
tion the young singer produces many more deplor-
able tones than when he was in the home pasture
and sang as a supernumerary in the local society.

Leaving the figure aside, this is true of the theological student. Under a considerable display of the
apparatus of exegetical science and surrounded
by the air of the initiated, he produces paralyzing
and unhappy trivialities, and the inner muscu-
lar strength of a lively young Christian is horribly
squeezed to death in a formal armor of abstract ideas.
If something more had been expected from the discussion afterward, even here, too, he develops an as-
tounding talent for jabbing paralyzing injections of
ideas into all lively, free, and easy conversation.

It is understandable that many churches are not
encouraged by such experiences to set great store by
theology as taught at the university.

4

The Theological Change of Voice

Now it is far from my purpose simply to accuse the theological student or to caricature him, although I grant that for reasons of illustration and of brevity I have spoken with a degree of kindly sharpness. What we are saying is due to two causes.

First, we are dealing with the quite natural phenomena of growth. Theological thinking can and ought to grip a man like a passion. But passionate devotion means a way of thinking and speaking which all too consistently is borrowed from the circles in which a person has just been moving.

In theology we are dealing with the form which reflection gives to spiritual experiences, as they have been developed through the centuries and especially by the great figures of church history. A twenty-year-old is taught, say, to think about the problems of the Trinity. Over these, down through the centuries, the most bitter battles have been fought with life at stake. To these problems the great leaders have bent mighty spiritual energies and behind them lie quite definite spiritual experiences. You can see that the young theologian has by no means yet grown up to these doctrines in his own spiritual development, even if he understands intellectually rather well the logic of the system — that is, its crust of what once was spiritual, and the legitimate and logical course, so to speak, of its developments in the history of doctrine.

Therefore it is evident how and where, given such a state of affairs, serious crises must arise. There is a hiatus between the arena of the young theologian's actual spiritual growth and what he already knows intellectually about this arena. So to speak, he has been fitted, like a country boy, with breeches that are too big, into which he must still grow up in the same way that one who is to be confirmed must also still grow into the long trousers of the Catechism. Meanwhile, they hang loosely around his body, and this ludicrous sight of course is not beautiful.

Spiritually the young student may perhaps be far enough along to begin to suspect and, as a Christian who prays, to know by practice, that in all our rebellion against God's demand we may still live confidently under his forgiveness and be free. But intellectually he is already beginning to think through the dialectic of law and gospel and Luther's paradox that man is both righteous and sinner at once (*simul justus et peccator*). Dialectic and paradoxes are the way a law-abiding church's thought overcomes the most monstrous frictions. They are the result of mighty, oft-repeated frustrations, abysmal anxieties, and wonderful moments of consolation.

The man who is in the position of reproducing a lecture about Luther, or possibly giving one himself, perhaps knows nothing or almost nothing about all this, and *can* hardly know. In his book on Goethe, Gundolf speaks, in reference to such cases, of a merely conceptual experience. Some truth or other has not been "passed through" as a primary experience, but has been replaced by "perception" of the literary or intellectual deposit of what another's primary experience, say Luther's, has discovered. Thus one lives at second hand.

But because this kind of perception of another's religiosity or spirituality can be extremely lively and even passionate, it is easy to lapse into autosuggestion, as if a person had experienced and passed through all that himself. He lapses into an illegitimate *identification* with the other. It is possible to be thoroughly bewitched intellectually by the mighty thoughts of the young Luther and then to lapse into the illusion that what is "understood" in this way and makes such an impression is genuine faith. In reality, it is only a case of perception and of being victimized by the seduction of conceptual experience. In his own life, in his own faith, the young man is not that far along! Young theologians manifest certain trumped-up intellectual effects which actually amount to nothing.

Speaking figuratively, the study of theology often produces overgrown youths whose internal organs have not correspondingly developed. This is a characteristic of adolescence. There is actually something like theological puberty. Every teacher knows that this is a matter of signs of natural growth over which there is no need to become excited. Churches must also understand it and must have it explained to them in every possible way.

It is a mistake for anyone who is just in this stage to appear before a church as a teacher. He has outgrown the naiveté with which in young people's work he might by all means have taken this part. He has not yet come to that maturity which would permit him to absorb into his own life and reproduce out of the freshness of his own personal faith the things which he imagines intellectually and which are accessible to him through reflection. We must have patience here and be able to wait. For the reasons I have mentioned I do not tolerate sermons by first-semester young theological students swaddled in their gowns. One ought to be able to keep still. During the period when the voice is changing we do not sing, and during this formative period in the life of the theological student he does not preach.

5

The Shock of Infatuation with Theological Concepts

In college discussions many of us have observed incidents which illustrate what we have just been saying. It makes no difference what university we are thinking of, whether it is Göttingen, Heidelberg, Erlangen, Tübingen, or Hamburg. For example, a young medical student has a question that he is eager to raise in the discussion period following the Bible-study hour. Under the pressure of putting it into words, because of his excitement and embarrassment, his pulse beats high. But finally he takes this pounding heart of his into his hands, stands up, frames his question and lets himself speak out freely with a couple of critical objections.

Now you should see how the young theological "pros" feel summoned to the lists. With lances lowered and at a rattling gallop, with their lips painfully locked, hardly repressing a howl of triumph, they pounce upon him. Then the technical terms fly around the uninitiated ears of the unhappy layman. Then rattle upon him words like "synoptic tradition," "hermeneutical principle," "realized eschatology," "prophetic foreshortening of the time perspective," "here and now," "ever and ever," "legitimate and illegitimate," "presupposition," and "toward what end," so that he hastily runs for cover, with one hand held up to protect his face and the other raising the white flag.

And so they easily suppose that this truce, owing to helplessness, is victory and that they have convinced the other man. But in fact, instead of winning him over, they have merely applied a kind of shock therapy — only it was never "therapy." They have smothered the first little flame of a man's own spiritual life and a first shy question with the fire extinguisher of their erudition. By such performances a person can really be smothered and strangled!

The medical student was in bitter earnest. Whoever is in earnest instinctively reacts with unusual sensitivity. And this instinct makes him say quite rightly: "Although my fate and my life were at stake, those others came at me with their routine. I found in them no trace of life or truths learned by experience. I smelled only corpses of lifeless ideas. I would rather go back to the less rigid young heathen. Granted that they haven't much to say to me, and that that little is probably wrong, at least it is genuine. I was looking for a Christian in whom I could detect a flame. I found only burnt-out slag. Maybe there was a glow underneath, but I am just so unused to it that I wouldn't see such hidden fire."

I know, dear students, that it hurts when I speak in such harsh and perhaps exaggerated terms. But I had to show you rather dramatically how seriously I regard my advice that you above all restrain yourselves with your theological concepts. It is certainly something to think about that student religious meetings are often much livelier and less cramped at the colleges and universities which have no theological faculties. You know me well enough to know that I am not questioning the value of university faculties — I am convinced of quite the opposite — but only that I am dealing with the problem of "theological puberty."

6

Pathology of the Young Theologian's Conceit

While we are dealing here basically with the most natural thing in the world, about which there is no reason to be excited further, looking at the matter from another angle it may well be that in the scenes we described at the beginning, where the first-year young theologian returns home, some symptoms of a real disease are appearing. It is possible — and laymen have a very exact perception in regard to this — that theology makes the young theologian vain and so kindles in him something like gnostic pride. The chief reason for this is that in us men truth and love are seldom combined.

It is also possible to say precisely why. Truth seduces us very easily into a kind of joy of posses-

humilty   humilty   humilty

sion: I have comprehended this and that, learned it, understood it. Knowledge is power. I am therefore more than the other man who does not know this and that. I have greater possibilities and also greater temptations. Anyone who deals with truth — as we theologians certainly do — succumbs all too easily to the psychology of the possessor. But love is the opposite of the will to possess. It is self-giving. It boasteth not itself, but humbleth itself.

Now it is almost a devilish thing that even in the case of the theologian the joy of possession can kill love. It is devilish because the truth of theology is concerned with the very love of God, with his coming down, his search, his care for souls. So the theologian, and not least the young theologian, gets into a horrible internal conflict. He is studying Christology, which means that he is busying himself with the Savior of sinners and the Brother of the lost. In connection with this he learns, shall we say, the Chalcedonian formula and the form-history of the Synoptics. And, in possession of this truth, he despises — of course, in the most sublime way — the people who as simple Christians pray to this Savior of sinners and cling to each of his — even perhaps legendary — miracles.

In his reflective detachment the theologian feels himself superior to those who, in their personal relationship to Christ, completely pass over the problems of the historical Jesus or demythologizing or the objectivity of salvation.

This disdain is a real *spiritual disease*. It lies in the conflict between truth and love. This conflict is precisely *the* disease of theologians. Like a child's disease, it is often especially acute. Even ordained pastors can still catch this disease without its power to do harm becoming diminished.

Some years ago a student from Tübingen got into a discussion about Bultmann with his landlord, a worthy and well-established pietist from Swabia. Quite understandably stirred up by Bultmann's reputation, the pietist saw in Bultmann the embodiment of evil. Now it so happened that the student was what is called a Bultmannite — a type, by the way, about whom the master would have fully as much right to be unhappy as Karl Barth and Ritschl about their corresponding Barthians and Ritschlians. It was no effervescence of genuine chivalry which prompted the student to defend angrily and zealously his badly misunderstood master. Rather it was a Pharisaic feeling of triumph, as he thrust into the hand of the man unfamiliar with Greek the Marburg professor's *Theology of the New Testament* underlined in blue and red.

His purpose unquestionably was to crush the man by the impression of an overpowering erudition to which he could never attain, and thus to reduce him to a feeling of helplessness. The combination of the pietist landlord's intellectual impotence and his agitation over heresies, which he was bound to regard as magnified all the more when underlined in red and blue, produced no doubt a very malicious joy in our student — and angered the pietist.

Nobody would maintain that this dubious pleasure of the student had even the least bit to do with Christian love for one's neighbor, not even in a much demythologized form. The purpose of his action was not to impart to the other man some understanding of what we theologians are driving at, or to lead him gently beyond the stage of his previous knowledge, but to render him helpless — this person who because of his previous education could not be equal to this literature set before him — and to suffocate his perhaps very simple objections to the historical-critical study of the Bible by throwing over them an overbearing and imposing blanket of arguments.

Here truth is employed as a means to personal triumph and at the same time as a means to kill, which is in the starkest possible contrast with love. It produces a few years later that sort of minister who operates not to instruct but to destroy his church. And if the elders, the church, and the young people begin to groan, if they protest to the church authorities, and finally stay away from worship, this young man is still Pharisaical enough not to listen one bit.

On the contrary, he glances triumphantly over the empty pews and says to himself: "Take thine ease, my dear soul, by thy truth thou hast produced a legitimate scandal and mayest regard thyself as justified," or even, "I thank thee, God, that I am not a rat-catcher or ear-tickler like those colleagues yonder after whom half the city is running. My empty pews testify on my behalf."

The brethren in actual pastorates who with undeviating fidelity are wearing themselves out on stony ground must forgive me for that last remark. I did not mean them, and they are made of quite different stuff. Just as babes can praise God, empty pews can testify to the fidelity of the ambassador, but in a very different way from that of those fellows with their vexatious dialectic.

7

The Wisdom of the World
as the Ally of Faith

The objection of ordinary Christians to theology must be taken seriously from yet another perspective. Besides the arguments from experience just described, there is also a certain skepticism on grounds of *principle*. Those characterized by this skepticism argue in this way:

In addition to faith, why should a special kind of knowledge be required to support it? Isn't it arrogance to suppose that only by the aid of critical penetration of the Holy Scriptures can substantial bedrock foundations be laid as the basis for faith? Doesn't this mean making worldly knowledge the schoolmaster of God's Word? Of course, put in this way, such an objection to theology is rather naively stated. But on that account we mustn't be prevented from discovering in it a real question that should keep our self-criticism on the alert.

If we ask why a scientific support for faith is required, by this question we may in fact miss the aim of our theological work. In general we have no desire whatsoever to undermine faith theologically. But we are wondering about what lies behind that objection of the "pious."

They are concerned about nothing other and nothing less than "faith alone" and "Scripture alone." They are suspicious of theology on the ground that it wants to temper the bold venture of faith by bringing on knowledge as its ally. They feel that "Scripture alone" is weakened because human criteria, such as intelligibility or reasonableness, are applied, and then the wisdom of the world takes precedence as the dominant criterion in the study of the Holy Scriptures. In this there may be some reminiscences of the forms of theology of the Enlightenment, which for the most part we have overcome, but the compromising tendencies of which are still affecting the unsophisticated to the third and fourth generation and beyond.

On the other hand, everyone who is initiated knows that these critical questions are never answered in any absolute sense. We must put them in a penetrating and uncompromising way to various figures among our contemporary theologians. For example, certain principles of interpretation in vogue today in the field of New Testament theology appear all too clearly to bear this stigma of worldly wisdom.

Furthermore, as we listen to these objections that are so naïvely formulated — that a last unassailable foundation will be analyzed away by the help of biblical criticism, that therefore in the Word of God there must be established a layer of what is credible, true history or rock-bottom gospel (kerygma) — do we not hear what Martin Kähler has compellingly said, with very much more fundamental and scholarly arguments, against the so-called method of critical subtraction? In his well-known book, *Der sogenannte historische Jesus und der geschichtliche biblische Christus* (*The So-Called Historical Jesus and the Biblical Christ of History*), Kähler called attention to two points.

First, faith makes sense only as unconditioned faith, because it has to do with our eternal destiny. It is impossible that it could be dependent upon and conditioned by the changing results of historical investigation or of scientific fashion. Second, Kähler has shown us that the person of Jesus Christ is not to be separated from his impact, that is, from the preaching animated by the Spirit and established in the church. The fundamental purpose of the gospel texts is therefore misunderstood if they are valued not as a testimony to faith but instead as records of biographical and historical interest.

In just the same way as every research method is determined by its subject, we must also take seriously the fact that the "subject" of theology, Jesus Christ, can only be regarded rightly if we are ready to meet him on the plane where he is active, that is, within the Christian church. Only the Son knows who the Father is; only the servant knows who the

Lord is. Apart from criticism of Kähler at particular points, about which we would say more, he has said here in a compelling way that history reconstructed apart from faith cannot possibly be the foundation of faith, and therefore that in no way can there be anything like scientific cooperation as a support or exoneration of faith, but that every theological effort is bound up with the act of faith itself.

8

The Instinct of the Children of God

To express this in another way, theology can never "prove" preaching, but it has the same outlook as preaching; it is also a witness, only with other methods and means. So its scientific character, its correct relation to its subject matter, its objectivity in the full sense of the word, is expressed only if it regards itself as a witness functioning through reflection. And this scientific character is not obtained by any ambition to include in theological study some chapters full of learned investigation "independent of faith." In any case this is certainly true of dogmatic theology. (To show this and to prove it in detail is, however, the task of dogmatic study.)

I should like to add to all this that the church has

the prior right to question us, even if it does not and cannot understand the details of our work; for we are pursuing our theological study in its very midst as surely as we are members of that church. Therefore these questions, even if they lack in detail some of the definite theological concerns that we entertain, may be highly relevant and constitute a fire through which we must always march. Ultimately these questions always have in mind our Christian life *behind* our theological reflections. *They are therefore questions about our soundness in the faith. The church is our pastor.*

Second, these questions must therefore be taken *seriously* and not liquidated by reference to the "mistakes in detail." For example, I personally have received mountains of letters asking me about demythologizing. Partly they are pervaded by a pitiful ignorance of what the problem is, and often, on that account, by a blast of the kind of pride usually connected — even among Christians — with that form of ignorance. But in spite of all that, they bear a trace of what I should like to call the *spiritual instinct of the children of God*.

I have always been conscious that this instinct is not to be despised, and that in the face of it I cannot evade my responsibility. I should like to ask you to place that instinct beside everything of a theological nature that you may perhaps be able to learn in this course, and to maintain a lively — even theological — dialogue with the ordinary children of God. Esoteric concealment on the perfidious ground that "I can't expect the people to be equal to this" could even lead to that offense against those least, for which Jesus coined the momentous picture of the millstone.

9

The Lofty and Difficult Art of Dogmatics

Theology, however, is not only an awesome thing, as it always appears to be in the eyes of the community of believers, but it is also an object of fascination. A well-known theologian once said that dogmatics is a lofty and difficult art. That is so, in the first place, because of its purpose. It reflects upon the last things; it asks wherein lies the truth about our temporal and eternal destiny. And the arc of this question reaches from the morning of the creation of the world to the evening of the world at the last judgment; it reaches from the least, the prayer for daily bread, to the greatest, the prayer for the coming of the Kingdom.

But dogmatics is a lofty and difficult art also because of its *subject matter*. It presupposes scientific and religious study of Bible texts, it ponders the thought of the Church over two thousand years, it comes to terms with philosophy and art, it broods over contemporary problems, and it inquires who man is with whom it currently has to deal and in what abysses he lives. Nothing human is foreign to it, if it is true dogmatics and not merely a rehashing recitation of Reformation and orthodox texts. Living dogmatics never allows its problems to be self-originated as by a virgin birth, but it is always being fertilized, achieving its productive impulse through the questions of the time. It exists in living tension.[1]

Moreover, dogmatics is a systematic discipline; that is, it attempts to include the whole of the study of revelation and to assign its details to their proper place in this whole. It is therefore, so to speak, completely antisectarian, for surely the mark of sectar-

1. See the chapter "What Is the Meaning of Dogmatics and Why Is It Studied?" in the author's book *Theologie der Anfechtung* (*Theology of Temptation*) (Tübingen, 1949).

ianism and heresy is that one member is lifted out of the whole body of teaching and absolutized, thus disfiguring the body by elephantiasis and in the end destroying it.

On account of this systematic purpose dogmatics possesses something like architectonic form. It erects a building the structure of which must be convincing, which betrays a certain logic in its construction, and which possesses a highly aesthetical charm even for people who have only a trace of feeling for cultural things. In my case I should regard as a boor any man who is not overcome by something like an aesthetic thrill in the face of the structure of Schleiermacher's *Dogmatics* with its connections lengthwise and crosswise, with its proportions and symmetries.

But if I now in a way praise dogmatics, if I speak of its magic charm and almost run the danger of being enthusiastic, again a decisive question is posed for our spiritual life. For this very charm brings us again, from another direction, face to face with the problem which earlier I characterized by the catch words "primary experience" and "conceptual experience."

While we are overpowered by a theological idea — let us say by Luther's idea of "saving judgment" (*servum arbitrium*), or Kierkegaard's teaching about paradox and indirect communication — we forget all too easily that we are being bewitched by the mere *form* of faith which comes to us in reflection. Our readiness to go along with this form of reflection and to let ourselves be swept up by it, though we understand it and are devoted to it, and are intellectually blessed, does not signify that we are carried away by fundamental faith itself.

It is possible to be bewitched by the landscape of primitive Christian thought, say by the long shadows which the world's evening sunlight, the approaching judgment of the world, draws upon this landscape. Thus it is possible to become an eschatological romanticist and an apocalyptic neurotic. There actually are cases of this, dear students, although tact forbids me to name for you examples of this sort. Such a person nevertheless has not comprehended a penny's worth of what it means to live on the battlefield of the risen Lord, between the first and second coming, waiting and praying as a Christian.

The talented, visionary, enthusiastic members of an elementary class in dogmatics are the very ones who swallow easily this magic charm of thought which dispenses with any real specific weight to the substance of its faith. That is why the discussions of theological students often seem weird to a man growing older. They make an impression upon him like that of a fight among shadows behind which there is no real bodily life.

10

The Hazard of the Aesthetic

I have wondered whether I should say this at all or keep it to myself. For I should not like to deprive spiritual combat of its freshness, neither would I like to see aesthetic and intellectual enthusiasm and the blessing of intellectual love of God replaced by the tired imagination of an old man, of which, I hope, you are not suspecting me! Permit me at this point to expose the intellectual hypertrophy of the theological aesthete — and who would deny that such types are found in many theological lecture halls? — as a very real disease, though at times it may be a wholesome fever.

My plea is simply this: every theological idea which makes an impression upon you must be re-

garded as a challenge to your faith. Do not assume
as a matter of course that you believe whatever
impresses you theologically and enlightens you intellectually. Otherwise suddenly you are believing
no longer in Jesus Christ, but in Luther, or in one of
your other theological teachers.

One of the most difficult experiences for a theological instructor to combat arises out of the fact
that good, respectable theology — by no means only
dissolute theology bristling with heresy — for the
reasons I have mentioned, threatens our personal
life of faith. Faith must mean more to us than a mere
commodity stored in the tin cans of reflection or
bottled in the lecture notebook, whence at any time
it may be reproduced in the brain.

Meanwhile, a completely new style of thinking
steals over us. We no longer say, as the man of prayer
does, "Lord Jesus Christ, Thou hast promised," but
we say, "The kerygma discloses to us this and that."
So long as this difference remains part of the technique of our theological handicraft, no objection
can be made to it. This technique needs the essen-

tial codes and the academic vocabulary previously agreed upon. In our work, so to speak, we cannot constantly be speaking in the language of the liturgy. But for how many people has not this difference meanwhile become something much more, a symptom of one's condition of faith or, rather, the loss of substance in that condition of faith?

II

The Study of Dogmatics with Prayer

The man who studies theology, and especially he who studies dogmatics, might watch carefully whether he increasingly does not think in the third rather than in the second person. You know what I mean by that. This transition from one to the other level of thought, from a personal relationship with God to a merely technical reference, usually is exactly synchronized with the moment that I no longer can read the word of Holy Scripture as a word to me, but only as the object of exegetical endeavors. This is the first step towards the worst and most widespread ministers' disease. For the minister frequently can hardly expound a text as a letter which has been written to him, but he reads the text under the impulse of the question, How would it be used in a sermon?

I have been a minister myself and say this also to myself. We might remember that Anselm begins his demonstration of God in his *Prologue* with a prayer, and that his dogmatics were therefore prayed dogmatics. This extraordinary fact would be understood altogether wrongly if seen as only an edifying preamble and therefore a sign of a special kind of piety. Anselm is here looking for nothing else than the expression of something that theologically is strongly relevant: a theological thought can breathe only in the atmosphere of dialogue with God.[1]

Essentially, theological method is characterized by the fact that it takes into account that God has spoken, and that now what God has spoken is to be understood and answered. But it can only be understood when I

(1) recognize that what has been said is directed to me, and

---

1. My course in dogmatics contains a chapter which deals expressly with Anselm's *Prologue*.

(2) become involved in formulating a reply. Only out of this dialogue is the theological method comprehensible (Galatians 4:9). Consider that the first time someone spoke of God in the third person and therefore no longer with God but about God was that very moment when the question resounded, "Did God really say?" (cf. Genesis 3:1). This fact ought to make us think.

In contrast with this, the crucified Jesus, out of the uttermost darkness of abandonment by God, does not speak to men, does not complain *about* this God who has abandoned him. He speaks *to* him at this very moment — in the second person. He addresses him as *my* God and even expresses his complaint in a word of God, so that as it were the circuit between him and the Father is complete. This observation, too, should make us think.

In the recent history of theology the same occurrence, namely, the transition from the second to the third person, is observable in that phenomenon called the history-of-religions school. Even if this is hardly to be found interpreted in this way in any historical presentation, the flattening and relativizing of the gospel is the consequence of a very subtle and at first hidden spiritual occurrence; the role of one personally addressed by the divine message is changed for the role of a neutral observer, and therefore in effect there is a transition from the second to the third person.

Further, I find a principle in the method of the writing of the history of theology — those who listen to my lectures know this — that not only the development of the forms of theological reflection, for example, the encounter with idealism, with existentialist philosophy, etc., is to be shown as a legitimate spiritual history, but that also theological reflection is to be understood as the precipitate of spiritual decision. I would consequently venture the definition: the history of theology is the history of Christians and their decisions made in faith presented in the form of reflections which are the consequence of those decisions.

12

Sacred Theology and Diabolical Theology

But if this is so, that is, if the weal and woe even of theological thought depends decisively upon the atmosphere of the "second person" and upon the fact that essentially dogmatic theology is a theology which is prayed (Wilhelm Stählin's language), then this naturally once more makes a claim upon our life as Christians. Whoever ceases to be a man of the spirit automatically furthers a false theology, even if in thought it is pure, orthodox, and basically Lutheran. But in that case death lurks in the kettle.

Theology can be a coat of mail which crushes us and in which we freeze to death. It can also be — this is in fact its purpose! — the conscience of the congregation of Christ, its compass and with it all a praise-song of ideas. Which of the two it is depends upon the degree in which listening and praying Christians stand behind this theological business. As a Christian, as a listening and praying Christian, each must fight not to be crushed by theology and thus, instead of being a Christian soldier, becoming a corpse on the battlefield.

Sacred theology therefore is not a word to be lightly taken upon our lips. Theology is a very human business, a craft, and sometimes an art. In the last analysis it is always ambivalent. It can be sacred theology or diabolical theology. That depends upon the hands and hearts which further it. But which of the two it is cannot necessarily be seen by the fact that in one case it is orthodox and in the other heretical. I don't believe that God is a fussy faultfinder in dealing with theological ideas. He who provides forgiveness for a sinful life will also surely be a generous judge of theological reflections. Even an orthodox theologian can be spiritually dead, while perhaps a heretic crawls on forbidden bypaths to the sources of life.

How all-important it is that a vigorous spiritual life, in close association with the Holy Scriptures and in the midst of the Christian community, be maintained as a background to theological work, and that the unformed shadows of thought always derive their life-blood from that source — all this becomes impressively clear to me particularly by the way in which historical-critical study of the Bible affects young theologians. Why is it that it often inflicts upon the young believers severe and sometimes deadly wounds, while we theological teachers are unable to spare anyone these attacks?

If a quite simple but fundamentally spiritual man, say an old pietistic fellow student or an emancipated member of the Hahn Community, has the questions of biblical criticism explained and is shown how the unity of the Bible's witness in the end is not destroyed by it, but how on the contrary the symphony of witnesses and the fullness of the message are only enriched, I believe that this will not shock him. Perhaps he might know that in fact he has been enriched.

13

On Theological Work in High Altitudes

It seems to me that there is a simple explanation for the fact that the effect of this knowledge at the age of students is frequently so entirely different and causes severe disturbances. Before the young freshman has really looked at the cornerstone of the biblical story of salvation, for example, the story of Creation and the account of the Fall, before he has come to know the Alpine peaks of the divine thoughts in their majesty, he is made familiar with the mineralogical analyses of that stone. But anybody who studies geological formations on maps and graphs, and learns mineralogical formulae from a set of tables before he ever climbs the Alps, is hardly in a position to comprehend at all what the Alps are.

I confess that to me one of the insoluble perplexities of theological study is that there appears to be no way — not for purely practical reasons! — to bring about the opposite and thus with it the healthy sequence of experiences. But it is all the more important to insist constantly and almost monotonously that a person who pursues theological courses is spiritually sick unless he reads the Bible uncommonly often and makes the most of opportunities by which, in preaching and Bible classes, that cornerstone is made visible.

Please understand what I have said as a preliminary exhortation. Unless during my teaching I knew that I had said this, I should have to reproach myself for a failure of duty, and I should not escape the crippling feeling that in spite of all my theological ideas that are perhaps unassailable — but I couldn't assert even that so simply — I would be leading you spiritually astray. You can listen to a course in theology rightly, that is to say, relevantly, only if you bring this corrective of simple listening and seeing to all the analyses of ideas.

We are working here as if we were in a mineralogical laboratory. But so far as the classification of knowledge is concerned, it is all wrong unless you yourself climb the mountains and breathe the air up there. We all know figures out of theological laboratories and ice-cold draftsmen whose breath is deadly. We are all threatened with drying up in laboratories instead of getting to the canopied heights and finding life there. In brief, it is in accord with the essence of theology or, as they prefer to say it today, it is theologically "legitimate" that the lecture room in dogmatics is filled with a congregation of Christian students.

I know, dear students, that it is unusual to begin a course in theology as I have done this time. But I had to put this little spiritual exercise at the start because my familiarity with a whole succession of listeners has constantly made me aware of the needs which can exist behind the study of theology, and also because I should like to justify myself in my work before the church of Christ. Just the year and a half that I spent with secular administrative duties, in which I could give no lectures, provided me with a perspective in which this situation became clear to me in a most compelling way.

The connection between the theologian and the spiritual man has come home to me with quite new strength. I hope that you, too, will notice this, even if we move over wide stretches in the sphere of abstract thought and if the exhortation to spiritual "hygiene" which I had to allow myself at the beginning is not repeated in quite this manner. If you will, keep these preliminary remarks in your memories as a motto to stand over all our work in dogmatic theology.